Belfast Boy

Belfast Boy

Chris Wright

© 2020 Christopher J.H. Wright

Piquant Editions
183 Platt Lane, Manchester, M14 7FB, UK

ISBNs

978-1-909281-66-0 Paperback
978-1-909281-64-6 Hardback
978-1-909281-64-6 Mobi

Christopher J. H. Wright has asserted his right under the Copyright, Designs and Patents Act, 1988 to be identified as the Author of this work.

All rights reserved. No part of this publication may be reproduced, stored in a retrieval system or transmitted, in any form or by any means, electronic, mechanical, photocopying, recording or otherwise, without the prior written permission of the publisher or the Copyright Licensing Agency.

Photo Credits: cover – Belfast City Hall: Giorgio Galeotti, Wikipedia Creative Commons; pg 6 – shutterstock.com: www.shutterstock.com/image-photo/senior-male-dairy-farmer-milking-cow-682491889; pg 7 – WikiArt.org: www.wikiart.org/en/claude-monet/haystacks-at-giverny; pg 12 – en.wikipedia.org/wiki/File:Attic_ladder_open.jpg; pg 13 – commons.wikimedia.org/wiki/File:Pushmower3.JPG, GURoadrunner / CC0; pg 17 – Alamy Stock Photo; pg 24 – iStock: www.istockphoto.com/gb/photo/old-football-boots-gm141573485-19565712; pg 29 – commons.wikimedia.org/wiki/File:London_bus_AEC_Routemaster_Park_Royal_SMK_726F_in_Garvagh,_Northern_Ireland_8_September_2007.jpg, Kenneth Allen / CC BY-SA (creativecommons.org/licenses/by-sa/2.0); pg 32 – Chronicle Live; pg 33 – Tottenham Hotspur: twitter.com/SpursOfficial/status/962295693154160640/photo/1; pg 33 – commons.wikimedia.org/wiki/File:Tottenham_Hotspurs_traint_onder_leiding_van_trainer_Michelson_op_bijvelden_Feije,_Bestanddeelnr_915-1564.jpg, Eric Koch / Anefo / CC0; pg 34 – Photo by Albert Bridge, CC BY-SA 2.0; pg 52 – Alamy Stock Photo; pg 53 – Alamy Stock Photo; pg 68 – www.pickpik.com/bible-holy-christianity-faith-book-closed-136368.

All Scripture quotations, unless otherwise indicated, are taken from the Holy Bible, New International Version®, Anglicised, NIV®. Copyright © 1979, 1984, 2011 by Biblica, Inc.® Used by permission. All rights reserved worldwide.

British Library Cataloguing in Publication Data
A catalogue record for this book is available from the British Library

Cover & Book Design: projectluz.com

For
My children and grandchildren

Contents

Chapter 1 1
    Irish farms and holidays

Chapter 2 9
    Our house and weekly visitors

Chapter 3 19
    Our family and a rusty sword

Chapter 4 27
    Our street and 'The Flying Menace'

Chapter 5 39
    Smells of my week

Chapter 6 47
    School days and old money

Chapter 7 63
    Into my heart

Chapter 1

Irish farms and holidays

'DADDEEE! HELP! DADDEEEE!'

I'm sure that's what I'm shouting, because I'm very scared. I've climbed right to the top of a large heap of straw and pig manure, and the crust has broken and I'm sinking down in.

And me in my new wellies, one of which is getting stuck and nearly covered in stinky stuff. They were probably red wellies, though I can't remember that for sure. But I know I am wearing wellies. Mummy put them on nice and new and clean when she let me out to play in the farmyard by myself. But they won't be much help if the manure gets over the top of them. Or over the top of me! Help!

I'm three years old, more or less, and this is the first thing in my life that I remember – sinking into a heap of yukky pig manure! I must have thought it looked a lot of fun to climb up that big pile. It looked like a mountain to tiny little me. But then it got all squelchy at the top. And now I'm stuck and sinking!

Daddy comes running out at last and rescues me. But he gets very dirty himself trying to reach me, so that makes him cross. But I'm just glad I'm safe again – even if my new wellies have to get a big wash to get all that pig poo off them. I'm saved!

We are on Lislea Farm in County Armagh in Northern Ireland. The farmer and his wife are called Mr and Mrs Mulligan and my father visits them often. They have two sons, Laurence and Oswald and lots of pigs – and so there's lots of pig poo and a lot of pig pong as well, as you can imagine. But I like that farm smell, and still do all my life, though cows do smell a bit nicer, and horses best of all. Pigs? – well, not really.

I like Mr Mulligan. He has curly hair, a big chest and very strong arms. And his hands are hard and rough. My Dad knows a lot of farmers around Ireland. One of them, Mr Fullerton, has such tough hands that he can pull out nettles without feeling any sting. That's really impressive, I think. But sometimes when you shake hands with a big farmer, they squeeze your hand so hard it hurts!

Mrs Mulligan is a bit scary and severe. At least she seems like that to me. She has long hair tied in a bun at the back and she gets little red spots on her cheeks when she is cross or excited about anything. Or when my Dad makes her laugh. Dad is very good at making people laugh. Even Mrs Mulligan, who doesn't seem to laugh much usually. But she gets red spots in her cheeks when she laughs at something my Dad says, or when he does one of his speciality whistles. I'm sure she's very nice really, but when you're as small as I am, you don't want to make her cross. She seems to be always in the kitchen, baking things, with an apron all covered in flour.

My Dad visits the Mulligans because they hold meetings in their farmhouse with some of their other Christian farmer friends and pray for the missionaries in Africa and South America and places like that. My Dad and Mum were missionaries too, in Brazil. But that was before I was born,

The lake at Ballyhamilton

so I only hear stories about what they did there. Dad's farmer friends like to hear those stories too, so he visits them and sometimes takes me with him.

Later on, Mr Mulligan arranged to have a great big tent in his garden for a special day once a year to hold the meetings in. Then my Dad holds meetings there and we all sing hymns and Dad preaches from the Bible and everybody seems very happy to listen to him. Dad does tell fantastic stories about his life in Brazil, on the River Amazon, and among the tribes people there.

We go on holiday to some other farms down in the south of Ireland too. My favourite farm is down at Ballyhamilton, near Enniscorthy in County Wexford. By the time we go there I have grown up a bit. Now I'm too big

Paddling my Mum round the lake

Sailing my yacht

and sensible to get stuck in pig poo any more! Now I'm a teenager and I'm allowed to do all kinds of things by myself. I love summer holidays in the south of Ireland on a farm.

This farm has a small lake with an island, a wee rowing boat and a kind of long punt. So I'm down there whenever

I like, swimming in the lake or rowing around in the boat, sometimes with the farmer's niece, June, who is about the same age as me. She talks with a strong southern Irish accent that I try to mimic. So I laugh at her accent, and she laughs at my Belfast accent. We tease each other a lot and make jokes.

June can speak Irish as well – that is, Gaelic, the old language of southern Ireland. We don't learn that language in the schools up in Belfast. She tries to get me to pronounce Gaelic words – but nothing sounds like what it's spelt like, and so she laughs at me again. I'm not sure I like being laughed at, but I do like her anyway, so it's good fun, out in the sun and in the boat on the lake. I love boats and water. Still do, all my life.

One day my Dad takes me out with the farmer's double-barrelled shotgun, to hunt pigeons and rabbits. The farmer doesn't like pigeons because they eat his crops, and he doesn't like rabbits because they eat his vegetables. So he shoots them both. Dad teaches me how to aim and shoot – holding the gun close to my shoulder and chin so it doesn't kick back and hurt. Dad used to have to shoot monkeys and wild boars for food in the Amazonian rain forest when he lived in Brazil, so he thinks he's back there! To my surprise (and in spite of my mother's protests), Dad allows me to take the gun out by myself in the early morning with a bag of cartridges, and after missing quite a few shots, I proudly come back with some rabbits and pigeons, which the farmer's wife turns into a very tasty pie. I don't think I'd be allowed to do that nowadays.

This is a dairy farm – lots of cows. I even get to milk some of them by hand into a bucket, though the farm does have mechanical milking machines. But it's quite exciting to sit on a little stool at the rear end of a big cow, watching out for her hind legs and swishing tail, and grab two udders with both hands and squeeze the warm and frothy milk down into a bucket. It looks like this.

And the farmer and his wife make their own butter from the cream. This is done in a marvellous old wooden butter churn, with a big crank handle. You spin it round and round for ages, with a splendid sloshing sound from the cream inside, until the cream separates into daffodil-yellow butter, and the white buttermilk that comes off it. And then the butter gets salted and patted with little wooden paddles into blocks like small bricks and wrapped up in paper or cloth. That butter tastes so delicious, especially on fresh home-baked bread with strawberry jam. But when my Dad puts too much butter on his slice of bread, my Mum scolds him, 'Joe!' she says in a telling-off kind of voice. Dad just laughs and teases her back. She thinks he's getting fat, but really, he's not.

Hand-milking a cow

We go there in the summer, when the long grass gets cut and dried in the fields to make hay. The country smells so beautiful when they cut the hay! Then I get to help the farmer rake it up into giant haystacks with big pitchforks. It doesn't get wrapped up in big black plastic bags, like you see in fields these days. It is heaped up into real haystacks to dry in the sun until it goes into the barn.

The best fun is jumping into and on top of the haystacks or hiding inside them – but you have to rebuild them or the farmer gets cross. Or, if the haystacks have already been formed and dried when we arrive, I help him using a hay-fork to hoist great loads of hay onto the trailer for storing in his barn for winter feed. That's hard work and I get blisters on my hands. But I like to think that the muscles in my arms and shoulders are growing bigger. All boys growing up want that to happen.

And then the farmer lets me sit up and drive the tractor and trailer round the field and back to the farmyard – bliss!

Another day my Dad decides I should learn to drive a car. I'm only 15, so I'm too young to learn on the open public road, but Dad reckons that a farmer's field should be OK. So he drives his car into the field after the hay has been cut and stacked. Puts me in the driver's seat and shows me the gears and how the clutch works.

Haystacks, by Monet

Then he gets out, and tells me to drive around the field as much as I like, steering around the haystacks and trees. It's great fun and great practice – starting and stopping and changing gears up and down and steering around the field wherever I want, whizzing around haystacks with inches to spare.

That's how I learned the basics of driving a car, until I got lessons from my older brother, Trevor, on real roads.

Where there aren't any haystacks.

As you may have noticed.

Chapter 2

Our house and weekly visitors

I WAS BORN, SO I'M TOLD, IN BELFAST CITY HOSPITAL, and lived for the first three years of my life in Fitzwilliam Street. I was born on 9th October, which is also my mother's birthday. 'You were Mummy's birthday present,' my brothers and sister used to tell me. And for a long time I used to believe them. I imagined that I actually got given to her wrapped up in fancy paper.

Fitzwilliam Street today

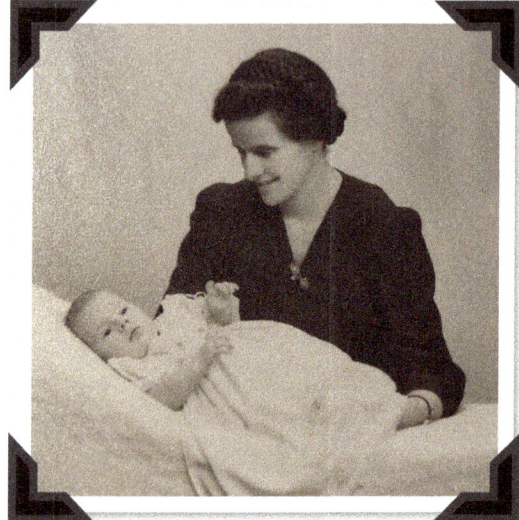

Of course, I'm too grown up to believe that nowadays! And anyway, here's a photo of me as a baby with my Mum, and I'm obviously not wrapped in fancy paper, but in an embarrassingly fancy white dress. My mother's name, by the way, is Mary, but everybody calls her by the name Maimie.

So my Dad's name is Joseph and my Mum's name is Mary, though everybody knows them as Joe and Maimie. Still, it's odd, isn't it? Joseph and Mary. Maybe that's why they called me Christopher, which means 'One who bears Christ.'

I have an older sister, Sheila (who was already 13 when I was born), and two older brothers, Paul (who was 10 when I was born), and Trevor (who was 5). So I'm the youngest, and my Mum keeps introducing me as 'her baby' – which is very annoying, since I'm not a baby any more!

Mum and Dad.
Maimie and Joe Wright.

But there's worse. Here's me with long blonde hair curling right down to my shoulders! Trevor used to tell me, 'That's when you were a wee girl.' And I believed him for a while! So I was a bit mixed up, don't you think? I thought I arrived on my mother's birthday wrapped up in fancy paper as a wee girl to start with! I think my Mum let my hair grow long like that because when I was born she actually wanted a little girl, and they were going to call me 'Evangeline.' So I'm glad I'm a boy and got the name I have. Can you imagine the nicknames other kids would have made up if I'd been called Evangeline!

Now we all live in a new house. It's number 129 Sicily Park, which is in Finaghy, on the southern edge of Belfast, on the way out towards Lisburn. It's a nice house, completely square with a small garden at the front, a larger one at the back and a garage. We came to live here in 1950 when I was three, but now I'm a bit older and I remember a lot about growing up in Sicily Park.

There are three bedrooms upstairs. At first, my parents were in the large front bedroom and Sheila in the small front one. So for a while all three of us

The house where I grew up

brothers had beds in the back bedroom – which was quite a tight squeeze. But then, my Dad got a man in to put floor boards in the attic and a skylight window. And also a ladder you can pull down from a trap-door in the ceiling to climb up there. It's a Slingsby ladder like this.

So Paul was given a mattress on the floor up in the attic and that became his bedroom. He climbed up to the attic every night. I was a bit jealous!

Eventually, Sheila got married in the same year when I turned 11. So Paul and Trevor share the back room and I've got the small front room, Sheila's old room, to myself, with the window over the front door. So Paul moved down from his attic to share the back room with Trevor, and the attic is now a great play space for me and other kids when they come to our house. I got a Hornby clock-work train set one year for Christmas.

So we laid out the tracks up there on the wooden floor that is much better than the carpet – and you don't have to clear them away every night! The attic is a great place to play, with nothing to break or be careful of.

On the ground floor there are two rooms. The one facing the front of the house we call 'the sitting room.' It has a sofa and armchairs, an electric fire, and a piano that my Mum plays. But we only go in there on Sundays, or on special occasions like if we have visitors, or at Christmas time. It has a different kind of smell – of hoovered carpet and polish. And it's usually cold, since the electric fire is 'too expensive' to put on for long.

Most of the time we use the room at the back, called 'the dining room', because it has a dining table and six chairs, two armchairs, a big sideboard, and a stereogram gramophone for playing musical records on. And best and most important of all, there is a coal fire in the dining room. So it's always nice and warm (provided the fire is lit, of course).

The kitchen has a back door opening out to a small paved yard. At the opposite side of the yard is a little concrete hut which used to get filled with coal for our fire. That was until my brother Trevor built another bunker along the sidewall of the yard for the coal, and then the coal shed became a cold store (it's always cold inside) for food and stuff. We call it the pantry. We don't have a fridge yet, though I've been in some of my neighbour's houses and they have fridges. So Mum puts food and milk and things outside in the old coal shed (pantry), or in the 'meat-safe' – which is a box screwed onto the wall in the coldest part of the yard, with a wire-mesh door to let the air in but keep the birds out.

Our back garden is just big enough to kick a ball around on the lawn. Dad loves doing that with us – and I can never get the ball off him. He's pretty good with a ball at his feet. And I'm big enough now as well to be able to push the heavy Qualcast lawnmower around to cut the grass (that's one of my jobs).

Building the garden shed

On one side there's a garage for Dad's car, and a wooden shed, that Trevor designed and built. That's him up on top, after a very posed photo of the rest of us!

And up the far end, two apple trees, a compost heap for the grass-cuttings, and a big hedge. I like our back garden, and play all kinds of imaginary games there. Over the fence on one side is the Brown family, with children around my age, and on the other side the White family (yes! All we needed was somebody called Green!).

At the front of our house we have another small garden, with a rose bed in the middle, a bed of peony roses, and Michaelmas daisies just outside the front door, which my mother loves because they bloom in the Autumn around the time of her birthday (and mine). One of my jobs is weeding those flowerbeds, which I don't really like at all, since Mum doesn't want even a blade of grass where only her flowers should be. And grass just keeps sprouting back, doesn't it? So it seems like a never finished job, which isn't fair.

Speaking of jobs, there are plenty to do around the house, and my sister and brothers and I have different ones to do in a kind of rota. One of Trevor's jobs is to polish the wooden floor of the hall, between the front door and the kitchen. He has devised a funny way of doing it. He throws me down on my back on the hall floor, with my sweater on, and then sits on my tummy. Then he tickles me so that I kick my legs. That has the desired effect of propelling me up and down the floor, making us both laugh and polishing the wood at the same time. Unfortunately, one day, he made me kick so hard and fast that I slid along and crashed backwards head-first into the front door. Which is made of glass panes in a wooden frame. My head smashed the bottom pane of glass to pieces. Somehow, it seems, I did not cut myself and Trevor probably got off with a spanking.

Alan White, my neighbour on one side, with a very attentive fielder

That front door gets opened a lot. Almost every day somebody calls for one reason or another.

There's the **postman** every morning, and sometimes just before lunch as well with 'the second post' – a rare thing nowadays. My Dad gets letters from missionaries in other parts of the world, so the postage stamps are sometimes very colourful and strange – from Brazil, or Congo, or Ivory Coast – all over the place. They make me think the world is very big and exciting. So I started collecting postage stamps quite early and now I've got several books full of them. It's amazing what you can learn about foreign countries when you get some of their postage stamps and then look up in your album where that country is and what it's like. It's a great hobby, and I use some of my pocket money to buy little booklets of stamps from dealers. Maybe that's why I love geography as a subject later at school. And just gazing at a map and imagining all the places on it. The world is such a wonderful fascinating place.

And then there's the **milkman** also every morning. Down go the full pint glass bottles with a clinky clank on our red door-step, and then the quieter clinking of the empty bottles that he picks up with all four fingers and carries back to his cart. I help him on Saturdays, as I'll tell you later.

Twice a week the **bread-server** arrives. He drives a small electric-powered van, with fresh-baked loaves of all varieties laid out on long drawers inside. There is a delicious smell when he pulls the drawer out to select a loaf. There's plain loaves and pan loaves, and baps and farls, and wheaten and soda – all different kinds of bread. My Mum likes the Ormo Bakery bread best, especially their 'veda bread', which is a yummy soft brown loaf. She gets the loaves she wants, and the bread-server man writes the prices down with a pencil in his book. Then Mum will pay him later or once a month when he comes round, with all the sums totalled up. I don't think any bakery has 'bread-servers' and vans these days. We all just go to the shops to buy loaves, don't we?

But my favourite is the **coalman**, who only comes every few weeks, to fill up our coal bunker. He drives a very black and dirty old lorry (well, it would be, carrying coal all the time). And on the back, on the lorry's flat base, stands a whole army of heavy hessian coal sacks, stuffed full with coal, and each weighing very heavy. The coalman, who is quite short but very strong, is also a bit black and dirty – his face streaked with sweat and coal dust under his flat cap. But I admire him so much when I watch how he handles the coal.

The coalman shoulders a big sack of coal

He wears a thick leather tabard across his shoulders and down his back to protect it. He backs up to the lorry, swivels a sack of coal around, and hoists it on to his back, holding it with his arms reaching back over his shoulders. Then he walks around our house, bent over under the weight, to the coal bunker at the back. And then, with a skilful twist, bend, and shove of his shoulders, he empties the whole sack out over his head into the coal bunker. SWOOSH and CLATTER it goes! And then he does it a few more times, depending on how much Dad has ordered to keep our fire going.

And then of course, there are the **bus-drivers**. Our house faces another street, at right angles off Sicily Park. And red buses go round that corner several times an hour. So they come very close to our house as they turn the corner. Not that the bus-drivers come to our front door of course, but one of them nearly did one day, and it scared me to bits, because it was my fault.

I have a bow and some arrows. Robin Hood is my great hero. I'd love to live in a forest and climb trees and shoot at the Sheriff of Nottingham. So one day, I'm sitting on the top of the gate pillar at the front of our house, and I imagine the red bus as the Sheriff of Nottingham's carriage. Just as it reaches the corner opposite our house and is going very slowly, I fire an arrow at it. It hits the side window of the driver's cab. The bus brakes very suddenly, right on the corner, and the angry driver starts to climb out his door. But before he gets his foot down on the street, I've dropped down behind the gate pillar, doing my best to hold my breath and hide. I hear him coming right up to the gate, shouting in anger. But to my amazement, he does not see me hiding behind the pillar, and walks away grumbling. And then I hear the bus driving off, and I let my breath out with relief.

I think I would have been in for another spanking if he'd found me and yanked me to our front door to confront my parents!

I don't think that ever happened to Robin Hood.

But then there weren't any big red buses in Sherwood Forest.

As I'm sure you know.

Chapter 3

Our family and a rusty sword

AS I TOLD YOU ALREADY, I AM THE YOUNGEST OF FOUR: elder sister Sheila, two older brothers, Paul and Trevor.

Trevor is five years older and bigger than me, and we quarrel a lot. I think he gets blamed for stuff, even when it's my fault, which is probably not fair on him, but I can't help it. I'm the youngest in the family and that has its privileges.

Our Dad is very loving and kind, but he does believe in giving us a spanking if we are naughty. Sometimes he uses his leather shaving strap (the strap he keeps to sharpen his razor; it's a bit like a belt for trousers only a bit wider), to give us a bit of a beating on our backsides. Well, maybe just two three whacks, but that's enough. Trevor seems to get it rather more than me. But he gave me good advice. 'When Dad gives you the first whack,' he told me, 'Don't hold your breath and pretend it doesn't hurt. Yell as loud as you can. Then he'll stop quicker.' That seems to work, and it doesn't happen often, and it's done me no harm.

One time though, Trevor actually nearly killed me. But since I'm writing this now, you know that he didn't. Here's how.

One day Trevor was down on Uncle Andy's farm (he was a relative of our Mum's), and he found an old sword way down deep in a big clump of bamboo. It was long and thin and rusty, and it might have been lost since the time of King Billy for all we knew (that is, William of Orange, who became William III, King of England in 1689, and fought some battles in Ireland). It certainly looks like something from the 17th century. Anyway, Trevor brought the sword home, and amazingly my parents let him keep it. In fact, Trevor still has it, in his house in Canada.

My brother Trevor with that sword

So one day Trevor and I were playing in the back garden and he was waggling the sword around like he was some knight of old. Suddenly he lunged forward, meaning to scare me, pointing the sword right at me. Of course he didn't mean to hit me, but I must have moved in the wrong way, and he hit me with the point of the sword on my forehead right between my eyes. It cut my skin badly and I still have small scar there if you look very closely. But if he'd hit my eye or my throat, I could have been blind or dead.

Which, as you know, I'm not. Thank God!

Now my sister **Sheila**, she's thirteen years older than me, which is really ancient when you're my age. She dotes on me, I know, but she says she was cross with me as a baby.

Apparently, she used to take me out in the pram on Fitzwilliam Street to show me off to the neighbours and passers-by. Then she'd coo-ee at me, and tickle my chin, to get me to smile for them, but I never would. She says I just stared up with a stubborn frown on my face and my wee chin stuck out. I still don't know why children are supposed to be all smiles and nice to strangers, but I've learned that's what you have to do anyway as a young boy like me, or else the grown-ups get annoyed. So I do try to smile to please them now. But when you're a baby, you don't have to smile at grown-ups just because they want you to. At least, I didn't then, for my poor sister Sheila.

Sheila took me out in a rowing boat once, on the sea at Bangor. It's another vivid memory from when I was about four years old – like getting stuck in pig-manure at three. I just remember that the boat seemed to be going farther and farther out to sea and we were all very scared we'd get drowned, and she had to row very hard to get us back to the beach.

So what with Trevor and his sword and Sheila out at sea, it's a wonder I'm still here.

Sheila has already gone to big school by the time I'm old enough to know anything, and soon she goes off to London to Bible College. When she comes back, she talks with a funny English accent, and she gets all upset when we tease her about it. But she's very musical, and maybe that's why she just picks up new accents. She has a lovely singing voice too.

And then there's **Paul**, who is ten years older than me. Paul's my hero. After Robin Hood, maybe. Or Davey Crockett.

One of Paul's jobs around the house is to light the coal fire every morning in the dining room – or to clear out the ash and put fresh coal on it, if it's been kept burning overnight. Making a fire is exciting, of course, so he shows me how to do it – and after he gets married it's going to be my job anyway. It's quite a ritual and there's a knack to getting it right. With all that central heating in houses these days, you probably don't know much about lighting a coal fire. Well, it's a regular part of my life as a child, so I'm going to tell you!

First of all, you have to clear out all the ash in the tray at the bottom of the fireplace, under the iron grate. That's dirty work, and it goes out in the bin at the back, or around the roses in the flowerbed. Then you screw up old newspapers into tight balls and stuff that on top of the grate. After that you take the firewood sticks and lay them carefully on top of the screwed up paper in a level criss-cross pattern. You need enough paper to light the sticks and enough sticks to make sure they will light the coal, and they need to be criss-crossed so as not to let the pieces of coal fall through too soon. It's quite an architectural structure in the end!

Then you place pieces of coal on top of the sticks – another dirty job – trying not to get coal dust on the carpet. Finally, you strike a match and light the lowest part of the newspaper. Don't go away, though! You have to wait to make sure that the sticks burn long enough to set the coal alight – and if that doesn't happen, you'll have to start all over again. So you watch the flames of the sticks licking around the pieces of coal until at last one or two of the coals start to spit and hiss and spew out little bits of smoke and then a small yellow flame, until at last you can tell that the coal itself is burning properly and the smoke is billowing up the chimney. Then you can pile some more coal on top, put the fire-guard in place, and let the room warm up, hoping that it's not too windy outside, which will blow the smoke back down the chimney and into the room. Cough, cough, and open the windows…

That fire is very important, actually. We don't have central heating or a gas boiler or anything like that (not for a long time). So at the back of the fireplace there are water pipes that are part of the plumbing of the house. So when the fire is lit, that heats up the water in the pipes and it gets stored in the tank upstairs. And when it's bath night (once a week), you just hope there's enough hot water in the tank for your bath. And there might not be if one of the family has had a bath before you. That's why we try to keep the fire burning overnight, damping it down with 'slack' – very small gravelly bits of coal that just smoulder for a long time. Sometimes the fire will last for days, and all you have to do is clear out the ashes underneath.

Of course, all the other houses on our street have coal fires too. And that means that sometimes there's a lot of smoke around in the air, which can be a bit of a nuisance, especially on windy days.

Have you heard of 'smuts'? Probably not. Well, when my Mum puts out the washing on the washing line in the back garden on a Monday, she's always worrying or complaining about smuts. Smuts are little bits of coal smoke that fall like bad-tempered black specks, and if they land on a nice white shirt or blouse, they make a real mess. If you try to knock one off, it just smiles and spreads. Nasty, and the shirt or blouse just has to go back in the wash.

But I was telling you about **Paul**. Paul goes to Annadale Grammar School and he plays rugby there. And when he leaves school, he goes on playing rugby for Annadale Old Boys. I love to go and watch him play, and I can't wait to play rugby myself, just like Paul, when I get to big school.

On Saturdays, when Paul comes home from playing rugby, I like to clean his rugby boots, which are made of thick leather right up and over the ankles, with big studs nailed into the bottom of the sole.

You have to scrape all the grass and mud off, wash them with a damp cloth, and then rub some Dubbin polish into the leather to keep it soft. Some day I'll have my own rugby boots when I get to big school.

Old rugby boots

But already I know all about rugby, all the positions of the players and the rules, and all the moves and scores – tries, conversions, scrums, lineouts, penalty kicks and all. I've tried explaining how the game of rugby works to my Mum. I got a piece of paper and marked out all the positions of the players on it. And I showed her how the ball gets passed from the scrum to the backs and so on, and I drew in arrows for the way the players would run, and then big crunchy X marks for the tackles. But she still says it doesn't make sense to her.

I keep wondering what position I'll play when I get to big school and can play rugby at last. Paul plays full-back (which is very brave of him, I think) or sometimes on the right wing since he's quite fast. When the rugby international season comes round, and Ireland is playing England, Wales,

Scotland, or France, we listen to the commentary on the radio (since we don't have a television) and I can imagine it all.

Sometimes on a Saturday afternoon, I take our transistor radio outside to the drive at the side of the house, where I wash Dad's car with a bucket of soapy water (another of my jobs), and listen to the rugby match at the same time. I have an older cousin, David Hewitt, who plays centre for Ireland, and for the British and Irish Lions, and we're all very proud of him. We go down to the Irish rugby stadium at Lansdowne Road in Dublin to watch him play. He can sidestep, and dummy, and kick, chase and catch, score great tries with his speed, and he's a really tough tackler. Just what you need in a centre.

David's brilliant!

But Paul's still my hero.

Chapter 4

Our street and 'The Flying Menace'

'CAN CHRISTOPHER COME OUT TO PLAY?'

That's what I love to hear from one of my friends in our street. And usually my parents say Yes. We all spend a lot of time outside playing, so long as we get our homework done before bed-time, and of course almost all day on Saturdays.

Our house is quite a long way up Sicily Park, at the other end from Lisburn Road which leads into Belfast. Our house is also on a corner of the street at a junction. If you look out of our front window, Sicily Park goes up a hill to the right, to a dead-end circle of houses, and down the street to the left to where some shops are, about 100 yards away. And from up the hill, there is a lovely view of the mountains, the Antrim hills, away in the distance. If we can see them, we know it's nice weather. If it's going to rain, the mountains are covered in cloud.

Our street, looking up the hill from the shops. Our house is the yellow one half way up on the right

Looking down our street from the hill at the top, towards the mountains

But straight in front of our house, at right angles to Sicily Park, is another street that leads up to a bus terminus. That's where the big red buses stand, at the end of their journey, before setting off back into Belfast.

For in fact, Sicily Park is at the end of the Balmoral bus route, number 58 or 59. So all day, every ten minutes or so, a big red bus comes round that corner in either direction. Either it's turning left at the end of its journey for its last stop at the terminus, or it's coming back and turning right into Sicily Park on the start of its journey back into the city. Which means, I suppose, that our house is quite noisy from those bus engines, but honestly we are so used to it that we hardly notice – except when visitors tell us they've been wakened up early in the morning by the first bus. But we just sleep on through!

Just like the buses in our street (except they weren't going to Trafalgar Square!)

It's very handy, though, to have the buses coming so close to our house. Since they are the old Routemaster buses, with an open deck at the back, you can hop off opposite our house just as the bus is going slowly round the corner, though the conductors (and my Mum) don't really like you doing that. But so long as you lean back a bit and are ready to run at the same speed as the bus, it's OK. At least, I've never fallen over.

When I go to big school, I have to get the bus every morning and come home by bus every afternoon. So the conductor comes around with his leather pouch for the coins, and his heavy ticket-punching machine, all strapped round his shoulders. The tickets are little pieces of thick coloured paper, that he tears off from the roll, depending on the price. And they all have numbers.

So the thing to do is look out for 'Readie-backs'. That means, numbers that read the same way backwards as forwards – like 51215, or 73137. The posh word for that is a 'palindrome' (just so you know). We collect those and are always boasting at school about having more than other boys.

Out on the street, the safest place to play is up the hill on the right. The buses don't go up there, and very few cars – since it's a dead end. And then, there's a piece of waste ground between the houses further down the street – great for hide and seek or cowboys and Indians, or cops and robbers, or bonfires and fireworks, and finding things in the brambles, or pushing people into the nettles. So – turn left or right, and our street has good fun places!

There are lots of boys and girls about the same age as me, and we do a lot of playing together. Next door are the Browns: Grace, John and Sheila. Grace and Sheila love skipping – with a big long rope that two of us have to swing around and around, while the others have to jump in the middle, skip up and down for a rhyme or two, and then skip out. It's not really a boy's thing, but they make John and me do it with them, so we let them. They say it's good exercise for your leg muscles. But it doesn't seem to do much for mine. I'm still far too skinny (at least that's what I feel).

I think I'm a wee bit in love with Grace Brown, though I'd never admit it. She says very nice things to me. Like when I get to big school and get picked for the Under 13s Rugby Team (the proudest moment of my life till then), she tells me she's not surprised because I try so hard to do things and that's why it works out for me. I hadn't thought of that before, but it's nice of her to say it. You get a warm fuzzy feeling when the girl next door says something nice and flattering. But I try not to let it show.

I also love Mr and Mrs Brown's house because they have a television set. Black and white, of course. My Mum and Dad don't think the TV is a good thing for children, so we haven't got one in our house. But they allow me to go to the Browns some afternoons to watch things on theirs. Our favourite is 'The Lone Ranger' – with his black mask, and his Indian friend Tonto and his big horse Silver – every episode ending with 'Hi-Yo Silver! Away!' And then there's The Cisco Kid and other Western series. But I still love playing Robin Hood with my bow and arrows the best.

Up the street are my other friends: Brian Walsh, Peter Thornton, Alistair McCorrie (who always has corduroy trousers that seem too big for him), Colin McCadden, and a few others. And then there's Jill Target. She's a bit older and has jet black hair and dark brown eyes. I reckon my brother Trevor is in love with her, for he keeps saying she looks fantastic (which I suppose she does if you're Trevor's age).

Friends on my street. That's me at the back on the right, with Peter Thornton. Colin McCadden is front right. I can't remember the other boy's first name but I think he was Jill Target's brother.

Now my Dad is a very good footballer. He used to play for a police team when he was on the police as a young man. And when we are out in the back garden, he can dribble a football around so cleverly that none of us can

A leather 'caser' football.

ever get it off him (which is actually very annoying, until he lets us get the ball!). I remember he was able to do that even when he was 60 years old (which is absolutely ancient when you're my age). So, even though I'm mad about rugby (for Paul's sake), I like football too (for Dad's sake).

So it was a great day when Dad gave me my own real leather football – a 'caser' as we call it.

I love it. I love the smell and feel of it. It is dark brown leather, with different panels stitched together, some of them quite soft like suede and some a bit shinier – but real leather! And it's called a 'caser' because that outer leather case has an inner rubber bladder (like a very thick balloon) that has to be blown up with a pump. So the leather has a slit in one of the panels, through which you can pull the neck of the bladder to blow it up. Then you have to fold over and seal the neck and stuff it back inside the leather. And then, the slit leather outer panel is pulled and tied together with a lace – a bit like your shoelace. When you're playing, you don't want to head the ball with that laced panel hitting you, for it hurts and leaves a mark on your forehead! And it's not good to play in the rain or wet grass, since the leather soaks up all the water and the ball becomes very heavy and hard to thump.

So, I'm the boy with the real leather 'caser' football! That's quite a status symbol in our street. A bunch of us get together and form a football team.

Danny Blanchflower of Spurs

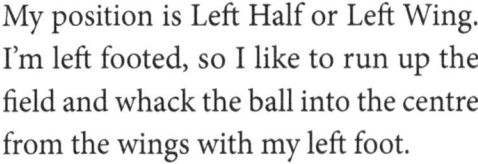

My position is Left Half or Left Wing. I'm left footed, so I like to run up the field and whack the ball into the centre from the wings with my left foot.

Now our big football hero right now is Danny Blanchflower. He's a footballer from Northern Ireland who is playing for Tottenham Hotspur, over in London (which is very far away, on 'the mainland', as we call Great Britain).

So we call our team, 'Sicily Hotspurs', and arrange a few matches with teams from other streets. There's a team up near where I go to school called the 'Benmore Rovers' and we play them quite often. Dad referees for us sometimes, though that's not always easy for me. When your Dad is the referee, you have to behave yourself! And it's so embarrassing if you miss the ball, or shoot it yards wide of the goal (which I do quite often). And don't dare use bad words when your Dad is referee!

But ever since then I've been a Spurs fan, as you may have noticed....

One day, Colin McCadden and I decide that we need to get a bit fitter, if we are going to really do well at sport. So we set off on a training run together.

Shaw's Bridge on the River Lagan. Photo by Albert Bridge, wikimedia.org

We head up to Barnett's Park, and then down to the River Lagan at Shaw's Bridge.

Then we set off running along the towpath, up river towards Lisburn. But since this is after school, it begins to get a bit dark. And we suddenly realise that we hadn't told our parents what we were doing. In fact, as it gets darker, we are too scared to go back along the towpath.

So we get to a bridge over the river and clamber up onto the road and hope we can hitch a lift in a passing car back to Finaghy. Just at that moment, to our great relief, my brother Paul comes along in his car and picks us up. He's been out searching for us. And he tells us that Dad is in his own car doing the same thing in a different direction. They must have been desperate, wondering what on earth had happened to us.

Well, when I get home, I've never known my parents so furious. If I thought they would be glad to see me safe back home (which I'm sure they were), that took a very second place to their anger at me for running away without telling them. I get a spanking, and get sent to bed without any supper – which is pretty hard, since after all that running, I'm starving. But I suppose I deserve it.

Back to our street.

Down to the left are some shops. There's the Co-op grocery and butcher's shop, a hairdresser, a chemist shop, and on the other side of the street there's a sweetie-shop and a newsagent, where I buy the Beano every week. All you need on one corner!

Best of all, there's a flat space outside the Co-op, between the shop and the road, which is great for roller-skating around on (until they spoiled it by building a wall around it). We love going there and whizzing around in circles and figures of eight, and chasing each other.

There is also a bus stop beside the shops, the first one after the buses leave the terminus up near our house. Now, at the back of the old Routemaster buses there is a number-plate, which is set in a bit from the back wall of the bus. There's a little overhanging ridge at the top of the number-plate. So if you sneak in behind the bus on your roller-skates, when it is stopped at the bus stop (making sure the conductor doesn't see you), you can grab hold of that little ledge with your fingers, and as the bus moves off you get pulled along the street at increasing speed on your skates, until you just have to let go (or the conductor hears and swats at you from round the back of his platform).

That's a trick we don't tell our parents about!

Up to the right of our house, our street goes up a hill to the dead end at the top. It's not very steep, but it's ideal for riding down on a bike, or scooting down on a scooter, or skating down on roller skates – just so long as you watch out for the buses turning the corner at the bottom!

But the best thing ever to come down it was **'The Flying Menace.'** That's the name of the buggy that Trevor and I built from an old pram. I say, 'was' because I'm sorry to say that in the end it all fell apart. But we gave it a glorious send-off, as I'll come to.

We found this old abandoned high-sided baby's pram that you don't often see these days. It had been dumped on the waste ground just down from our house. It was dark blue on the outside. It had a nice cream-coloured padded interior, and four really big wheels that made it bounce up and down.

The Flying Menace was like this, but had the upper part of the pram as well.

Well, first of all we took off the front two wheels. Then we screwed a long wooden plank to the underside of the pram. Then we attached the two front wheels and their axle up underneath the far end of the plank out at the front. We did it with a bolt through the middle of the plank that meant the wheels could be turned a bit to the left and right. Then we tied a rope around each end of the axle, like reins on a horse, so that when you sit in the pram you can steer the whole thing by pulling on the rope left or right.

It's brilliant! And because the wheels are large, it can bounce along at great speed, even over kerbs and bumps. There's a kind of brake handle on the side too, that rubs on the tyre of one of the back wheels. So you can slow it down a bit but not much more – provided you can spare one of your hands from the steering rope to operate the brake – all a bit risky!

So we pull it up to the top of Sicily Park hill, and then race down gathering speed, with one of us sprinting alongside, hoping to turn smoothly onto the pavement at the bottom and into our driveway. But half the time if you steer too hard to left or right the whole thing tips over and you tumble head over heels with it. I suppose that's why we called it 'The Flying Menace' and painted that on the side. And if you see a bus coming round the corner, a hard turn and tumble is better than an argument with the bus!

Well, it gave us a lot of fun and plenty of cuts and scratches too. And some Saturdays I used to pull it along to pick up wooden boxes from the grocery shops, that I chopped up into firewood and then sold in bundles around the streets.

Eventually, however, it fell apart and was too broken for us to fix. So we dragged it sadly back to the waste ground where we found it. There we filled it full of bits of wood and rubbish that would burn. Then we put a few big potatoes in it as well, and set fire to it. It made a great, if rather tragic, bonfire. And afterwards we celebrated by eating the nicely baked potatoes that we dug out of the ashes.

'The Flying Menace' would fly no more.

Chapter 5

Smells of my week

DIFFERENT DAYS HAVE DIFFERENT SMELLS. I sometimes think I can tell the day of the week by the smell of it.

Mondays smell of soap and washed clothes on the line. That's the day Mum does the family washing. She does it in the washing tub in the kitchen, and so the house all smells of the washing powder. The machine manages to do a wash and then a rinse, but it doesn't have a spinner to get the water out. Instead, it has a mangle on top. That's two heavy rubber rollers with a great big crank handle. If you push wet clothes through the mangle and turn the handle, the rollers squeeze out as much water as you can. Then she hangs it all up on the washing line out in the back garden, and hopes it won't rain, and smuts won't come down from the smoke.

Tuesdays smell of mud and grass. That's because when I get to big school, Tuesday afternoons are for

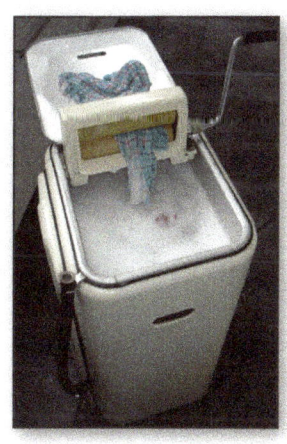

Washing machine and mangle

games – and I get to play rugby at last! So we have to walk from our school quite a long distance across Belfast to Pirrie Park on the Ravenhill Road. That's where the school's sports grounds and pavilions are. The pitches are good, but if it rains, they are very muddy. And rugby in the mud and rain in the middle of winter is not much fun at all – even though I do love the game. Grass and mud have a great outdoors smell in the rain, though the smell of the changing rooms afterwards is not so nice!

Big school for me was the Methodist College Belfast, MCB, or 'Methody' as everybody calls it. When I first arrive at big school I'm not very 'big' myself – in fact, to be quite honest, I'm rather small and skinny and desperate to grow a lot bigger. I'm still only 11 years old.

Leaving home on my first day at Methody

Methody, my big school. It has a lot more modern buildings as well.

Well, the first Tuesday games afternoon, all us first form boys are out there on the rugby pitch, in our new navy blue shorts and rugby shirts and boots. And the sports master (Mr McConkey, or 'Conkers' as his nickname is) is deciding what positions to put us in. He takes a look at me, a lot smaller than two of the big boys, and says, 'OK Wright, you'd fit in between them nicely, so you can be Hooker.'

So that's where I end up playing rugby – as Hooker in the front row of the scrum, in between two big boys who were Props. And my left foot comes in useful too. For my job is to hook the ball out when the Scrum-half puts it into the scrum, and I'm pretty fast at shooting that foot out, whether the ball is coming from the left (my own side), or the right (when it's the other side's scrum). So I win a lot of balls 'against the head' – which pleases the teacher and my own side, and I try not to be proud of it! Plus, being in with the forwards is a lot warmer on a cold windy wet winter's day than standing out on the wing!

The rest of the week just smells of school – books and pencils, toilets, left-over half empty bottles of free milk, school dinners, raincoats, that teacher who needs a deodorant, and other kids…

Sundays smell of mothballs. That's because we have to wear our best clothes to go to church. And my Mum keeps her Sunday best dresses and coats in a wardrobe with mothballs to keep out the moths. In fact there are mothballs in all our wardrobes, so Sunday best suits and coats all smell that way.

Mum even has a **fox-fur** over her shoulders, and that smells the worst of mothballs. The story is (and I think it is true) that the poor fox was killed by my Dad's car out in the countryside one night. So he picked it up and took it to some man who had it skinned, and then lined its fur with cloth and turned it into a kind of reddish fur shoulder shawl or stole. And my Mum wore it to church on Sundays.

It's a bit weird, I think, though I'd never say so to Mum. I mean, would you wear a dead fox round your shoulders? Didn't think so. The fox's little nose and eyes (glass, of course) point down my Mum's back, while it's little legs and paws have clasps that fasten round her front. I don't know what the people who sit in the pew behind us in church think of having a glass-eyed fox staring accusingly at them all through the service.

I don't expect the fox is giving a lot of thanks and praise to the Lord either.

Mum's fox shawl looked a bit like this.

My milk cart was one like this

Saturdays smell best of all! There's the wild smell of the great outdoors, of our street in the sun or rain, my leather football, things in the garage to play with, fix or mend, fresh windy sunshine and clouds, Balmoral buses, my old sweater and Saturday play clothes, the Beano, cut grass on the back lawn, nettles and dock leaves on the waste ground, the smell of the shops (fresh vegetables in the grocery, fresh sawdust on the floor of the butcher's, sugary smells in the sweetie shop), and shoe polish (we have to polish our shoes for Sunday on a Saturday night).

Saturdays are full of stuff! Stuff that all smells of fun and adventure and freedom from school.

One of my very favourite things to do on Saturdays is to help the milkman with his round. And that's because he drives a horse and cart. Boyd's Dairy is just the other side of the Lisburn Road, and they still use horses and carts to deliver milk around the streets of Finaghy.

So as early as I can on a Saturday morning, I run off to find him. He lets me jump up beside him on the cart, and a lot of the time lets me hold the reins, giving the horse the commands to walk on, or to stop, each time we have milk bottles to deliver and collect. So I hop down, grab a few full bottles and go to the front doorstep of each house, check if there's a note in an empty bottle telling the milkman how many bottles to leave today, put that number down, collect the empties and hurry back to the cart.

After doing that for a few hours, or when he's finished his round, the milkman gives me half-a-crown. That's a nice big silver coin worth two shillings and sixpence, or 'two and six' as everybody says. In today's money that would be twelve and a half pence. I'll tell you about old and new money in the next chapter. For me, half-a-crown is a lot of pocket money, and the first thing I go and buy is my comic, the Beano, for threepence. And in the sweetie shop you can get eight black-jacks for a penny (that's a liquorice sucking sweet that's very nice). Now half-a-crown would be the same as thirty old pennies, so that would be a lot of black-jacks!

But of course I don't spend all my pocket money on sweets. You wouldn't either, would you? Course not!

If I've time, I can earn a bit more money. I go to the Co-op shop and ask for any old wooden boxes that have been used to deliver fruit during the week. They usually have plenty, and are happy for me to take them away.

I smash them as flat as I can and I drag them back to our garage. Then I grab a hatchet, and chop the boxes up into firewood sticks, for kindling the coal fires that everybody has. I tie the sticks up into small bundles with string – some larger, that I can sell for two pence a bundle, and the smaller ones for a penny a bundle. Then I'm off round the streets, pulling the firewood in the Flying Menace, while it was working, and offering my bundles for sale at every door. Most people take some – probably out of pity! So I come back with a pocketful of pennies, threepence and sixpence bits, to add to my half-crown. I might buy some more stamps with that for my collection.

And for a while, on Saturday mornings, there's another thing that happens in our garage. A bunch of my friends from the street, our next door neighbours' kids and some from the Sicily Hotspurs, come round to our garage and we have a 'wee meeting'. As I said before, my Dad is a preacher and so I often go to meetings with him in churches and halls. So this kids meeting in our garage is my own wee way of following in his footsteps, I suppose. Anyway, we sit on the floor and sing some choruses and I read something from the Bible and make a wee speech about it and then we say a prayer and finish. Sometimes my Mum or Dad come in, but mostly I lead it by myself, and then we run off to play somewhere. I suppose it's us kids doing something we see grown-ups do in church. But my best friend next door, John Brown, became a follower of Jesus at one of our 'wee meetings' and he still keeps in touch with me.

After I go to big school, a lot of Saturday mornings are taken up playing rugby for my school team (the Under 13s XV) – either 'at home' in Pirrie Park, or 'away' at some other school in Northern Ireland. And then of course, you never know what the boys in the other school's team will be like. Sometimes they seem an awful lot bigger than our team is. Certainly a lot bigger than me anyway.

Mr McConkey tries to encourage us. His favourite words to us, when we're getting changed before a match, are, *'Remember lads! The bigger they come, the harder they fall!'* That's supposed to fire us up to tackle them fearlessly when they charge at us at the kick-off, or come running at us full speed with the ball. He doesn't convince me, though, since I'm a bit small and skinny (have I mentioned that?).

My rugby team when I was in the Under 15s. All trying to look hard and fierce! I'm second from the left in the back row.

That's why I admire my brother Paul so much, playing at full-back, where he has to tackle other players on his own all the time. That's definitely not where I'd want to be! I'm OK being up the front with the other forwards where we all sort of tackle and wrestle and grab and shove together.

As far as I'm concerned, the bigger they come the harder they hurt!

Chapter 6

School days and old money

BLACK SLATE AND WHITE CHALK and Leslie's check-coloured shirt.

That's what I remember most about my first day at school. I've walked round all the streets from our house with my Mum to Finaghy Primary School, in Benmore Drive, and she leaves me there for the morning. Most days I go home for lunch. At first she collected me, but now she says I can walk it by myself.

The teacher gives us each a small black slate tablet and a stick of chalk. I'm not sure what to scribble on it, but it's fun anyway. Later on we get paper and pencils, but I always remember slates and chalk at the start of my school career.

I've been put to sit beside another boy called Leslie. He's got fair hair like me, and a

My friend Leslie

Finaghy Primary School, as it is now. It's got new gates since I was there!

Benmore Drive, where our football rivals, the Benmore Rovers come from.

very bright check-coloured shirt. Funny how I remember that. We get to be quite good friends, since we sit together a lot.

Later on, when we're learning spellings, we are having a test. The teacher calls out words and we have to write down the correct spelling – if we know it. Well on this day, I know I'm getting them all right until she calls out the word, 'People'. Now I'm stumped. I know it's got a funny spelling, but I can't remember what it is. I mean, why has it got an 'o' in the middle?! (Actually, now I know the reason for that. It comes from the Latin word 'populus' for people). Anyway, I can't remember the right spelling. So I write 'peeple'. But I'm fairly sure that's not right.

And then I do a naughty thing and look over at what Leslie has written, and he's spelt it properly – 'people.' So I cross out my wrong answer and put the right one in. And I feel very guilty about that. I'm old enough to know already that it's cheating and wrong to copy somebody else's work and pretend you got the answer right when you didn't. I'm sure I'll do a lot more wrong things in life than cheat at a spelling test, but it sticks in my memory even as a child that I sort of told a lie on paper.

And telling lies is a bad thing, isn't it? I know God isn't pleased with that.

We get a milk break every morning. The milk comes in little glass bottles that are one third of a pint, and you have to drink it through a waxy paper straw that I don't like. And by the time of morning break, the milk is often a bit warm. And sometimes empty bottles get left or forgotten under a table or on a window ledge (or worst of all, on top of a radiator), and then they don't half smell bad!

Some days we get orange juice as well. It has a concentrated kind of flavour, not fresh juice. I think it's because we all need extra vitamins to help our bones grow properly, or that's what I've been told. The government wants us children to grow up more healthy than they did during the war. That's the Second World War, which ended in 1945, so I am among the first generation born just after that.

So at school we do all the usual things like reading and writing and doing sums and learning the 'times tables'. We have to learn our number tables right up to 12 times (like 12 times 7 is 84. Or 12 times 12 is 144).

And the reason for that is – money. Because until I get to be a grown up, all the money in my childhood is in pounds, shillings and pence. Now I'll have to explain that.

You know that today money is very simple. You have one pound. And every pound is divided into one hundred pence. That makes adding up or subtracting very simple, because your pound column and your pence column all behave in the same way. You're thinking and counting in tens. 10p, 20p, 30p, 40p, 50p, 60p, 70p, 80p, 90p, one pound, and so on.

But in the old money:

- One pound was divided into twenty shillings.
- And one shilling was divided into twelve pence.

So   12 pence = 1 shilling
And 20 shillings = 1 pound.

Each column for adding up money was headed **L** (for pounds) **S** (for shillings), and **D** (for pence). Which sounds even more crazy. Actually, those three letters all came from the Latin words for those amounts – thousands of years ago! *Libra*, *Solidus*, and *Denarius*. L. S. D. – see? But we just say, 'Pounds, Shillings and Pence'.

L S D. = Pounds, shillings and pence. That's the old money. Got it?

So you have three columns to add up (or take away, or multiply or divide). Here's an example.

L	*S*	*D*
3	17	6

That means 3 pounds, 17 shillings and 6 pence.

It would be written £3-17-6. And you would speak it as, 'Three pounds, seventeen and six.'

Or let's say £49-13-11. You would say, 'Forty nine pounds, thirteen and eleven.'

And if it was less than one pound, it might be seventeen shillings and sixpence. That would be written 17/6, and you'd say 'seventeen and six'. Or five shillings. That would be written 5/- and you'd just say, 'Five bob'.

Now suppose you have to add up

L	S	D	
3	17	6	(Three pounds, seventeen shillings and sixpence)
5	9	11	(Five pounds, nine shillings and eleven pence)
7	13	10	(Seven pounds, thirteen shillings and ten pence)

You have to count the Pence column up to twelves, and carry forward the shillings. And then you have to count up the Shillings column to twenties, and carry forward the pounds. Do you want to try?

So the right answer is:

L	S	D	
3	17	6	
5	9	11	
7	13	10	
17	1	3	(seventeen pounds, one shilling and threepence).

Have a go at doing longer sums in **L.S.D.**, and try to imagine what it was like adding up big long columns, or doing take aways, like when you have to make sure you are getting the right change in a shop!

So the shop says that your bill comes to £3-15-9. That means three pounds, fifteen shillings and nine pence. And you give the shopkeeper a five pound (£5) note. How much change should you get back?

(Did you get it right? It's £1-4-3: One pound, four shillings and three pence).

Or even worse, multiplying and dividing!

Why not make up some columns of old money in **L.S.D.** and try adding them up. Remember, your D column for pennies can only be 0 – 11, and your S column for shillings can only be 0 – 19.

And of course the old money had its own notes and coins. There was a green one pound note, and a red ten shilling note. Here are some photos.

A one pound note

A ten shilling note (worth 50p now)

These are the coins that I have in my money box.

- Half a crown   (two shillings and sixpence; eight of them in a pound)
- A Florin   (two shillings; ten of them in a pound)
- A shilling   (twenty of them in a pound; also known as 'a bob')
- A sixpence   (two of them in a shilling, also known as 'a tanner')
- A threepenny bit   (four of them in a shilling; usually called a 'thruppeny bit')
- A penny   (240 of them in one pound)
- A halfpenny   (pronounced like, 'heypnee')
- A farthing   (a quarter of a penny). But that stopped being used when I was about 12 years old.

The old coins

Sometimes I go with my Dad to meetings were money is collected for the church or for missionaries. He lets me help him count up all the coins, while he does the notes. Counting those coins is quite a complex system!

- You pile up the pennies and halfpennies into twelves, to make shillings or sixpences.
- You pile up thruppenny bits in fours and sixpences in twos to make shillings
- You pile up shillings into tens, and two of those piles make one pound.
- You pile up the florins into tens, to make one pound
- You pile up the half-crowns into eights, to make one pound.
- Then you start counting the piles! You need some paper to write down all the amounts and then add them up.

And yet, somehow, it was all just the way things were. You learned to count in tens, twelves and twenties, and you knew how to read all the prices in shops and the bus fares, and you just made sure you gave and received the right amounts.

In fact, some people say that twelve is a more useful number than ten, because ten can only be divided once – by two. Whereas twelve can be divided in four ways – by two, three, four and six.

That's enough about money, I think. And sums. You should be glad you live after they changed to the decimal system!

Back to my school.

The best girl in our class is **Etta Stretton**. That's a funny kind of name, until I'm told that her first name is actually Henrietta and she just shortened it. She's very clever and gets top marks. She's also very pretty and everybody likes her.

And the best boy in our class, at sports anyway, is **Brian Dean**. When we play games in the playground, his team is always the best at whatever we do, and we all want to be on his side. He's also a very fast runner. I have never managed to beat him in a race on any of our sports days. There's just one thing I *can* beat him at, and that's the high jump. I don't know why. Maybe it's because I've got spindly long legs, or that I've always been fascinated by monkeys and wish I could leap and swing around in the trees like them.

Oh, there is one other thing I usually win at, on sports days, and that's the four-legged race. I don't know why, but I'm able to 'run' quite fast on hands and feet (not hands and knees!). Maybe that's because (as I think I may have said already), I'm a bit skinny and spindly. But the four-legged race is just something everybody laughs at. Like the sack race. Or the egg and spoon race. Not exactly an Olympic sport, is it? No prizes for winning it. So that's why I am at least happy to be good at the high jump.

But my best friend at primary school is **Maurice Judge**. Mind you, he wasn't always my friend. In fact it all started rather badly. We didn't like each other at first, not at all.

And one day, in the playground, we get into a fight. I can't remember what we are fighting about, but I've gone quite wild. I 'see red', as they say. We're punching and grabbing each other and rolling around on the ground – which is tarmac, so we are getting cut as well. And other kids gather round like they do, shouting 'Fight! Fight!'

We each give as good as we get, with bleeding noses and cut knees. And then, with all the commotion, the headmaster comes out. His name is Mr R.E. Brown, and he is very strict and fierce. He grabs us both and hauls us back inside, for a real telling off. We both get the cane – which is not allowed nowadays in schools, but was quite often used in my school. That is, a springy piece of bamboo that was used to whack you on your open hand, or on your bottom. He gives us a good thrashing. And then he gets us washed up and sent back to class, and to detention.

Maurice Judge (centre), with two other friends (Trevor and Greg) on our last day at Finaghy Primary School, when we didn't have to wear school uniforms.

And, amazingly, Maurice and I become best friends after that! That's hard to explain. But maybe it was because the fight sort of ended in a draw and we both got punished as we deserved to, that we become comrades. So we go and play together on Saturdays and have a lot of fun and adventures.

But that's when something else happened that I felt quite ashamed about.

Maurice lives up in another part of Finaghy where there is a lot of open ground, and also an exciting bit of woodland. The only trouble is, those woods are on the other side of a railway track. Railway tracks were not all fenced off in those days. And when we were on our holidays in a place that was also near a railway track, Mum told me very severely that I must never walk on railway tracks. Which I think you'll agree was a very sensible rule to make. Like, I mean, *really* sensible.

But those woods over there are so enticing! We could have such adventures in there, making dens, playing Robin Hood, and all that. So, I tell Maurice *to carry me across* the railway tracks on his back, so we could go and play in the woods. That way, if ever Mum asks me if I'd walked on the railway tracks, I could say 'No, I didn't.' And I'd be thinking to myself 'No, I didn't actually *walk* over the tracks; Maurice carried me.' Which of course was only a half-truth, and would really have been another lie. And I'd be deceiving my own mother, as well as disobeying her! Well, actually, Mum never did ask me, so I never had to say that. But I know that if I *had* said it, I would have been telling a lie, for doing something that I knew I was not allowed to do – cross over the railway tracks. Mind you, I think she would have known that I was lying, and I'd have been in really big trouble. Remember my Dad's shaving strap?!

Sometimes we can be so clever at thinking up ways to disobey the rules! But being clever is not the same as being good, or sensible, is it? In fact, looking back now, I'd say it was not only naughty of me to do that, but very stupid. And very dangerous. It's good that railway tracks nowadays are fenced in. To keep out stupid and naughty little boys like me.

But that was me and Maurice.

Most of my other friends, as I said, are our neighbours in Sicily Park, our street. So they are the ones who come round for things like my wee garage meetings, or birthday parties. We get dressed up for parties, like even wearing shirts and ties!

I mentioned school holidays, which of course are the best part of being at school!

My 11th birthday party.
That's my cousin Andrew on the left.
Note the ties!

As well as those farms that I mentioned in chapter 1, there is a place near Newry in Northern Ireland that my Dad and Mum take us for a week or more in the summer. It is a small school with the head teacher's house attached. And when the head teacher, Mr Wray, goes on holiday himself, he lets us stay there in his house. It is in the countryside, and there is a railway line running alongside the school wall (that's where Mum told me never to walk on it – and I didn't, not there!). But just beside that wall is an enormous ancient sycamore tree. And I love climbing trees!

I imagine myself as a monkey, or as Robin Hood, and I go up there nearly every day, finding new ways to clamber all around it, higher and higher. I know the rules for safely climbing a tree. I'm sure you do too.

- always make sure that a branch is good and strong before putting your weight on it;
- keep close in to the trunk of the tree as much a possible, where branches are stronger;
- never hold onto a dead branch;
- always have three out of your four limbs (two hands and two feet) well attached as you move a hand or foot to another branch, and so on.

It's safe enough if it's a good strong tree and you move carefully and don't jump around (since we aren't actually monkeys!).

And one of the great things is that from up the tree I can see all the way along the railway line for miles, as it stretches right away down over the border into Southern Ireland. And that means I can see trains coming for miles and miles, the great steam trains, with all their smoke and steam puffing out. And then they thunder past just under the tree and it's like everything shakes until it all goes quiet again as the train disappears up the track in the distance towards Belfast. I love climbing up the tree in time to watch for the trains.

A steam train near Newry. I obviously wasn't up my tree at the time!

Dad, Mum and Trevor, at a picnic at Shilling Hill beach.

Not too far away is a beach at a place called Shilling Hill, and we go there for picnics, if the weather is even half way warm. The Irish Sea always feels very cold, but I love being at the seaside, and all the fun you can have in the water and on the beach. All my life I've loved swimming in any sea I can get into! But since I'm still such a skinny wee fella, I get cold and shivery and turn blue a lot of the time, until Mum insists I come in and get wrapped in a towel or rug, and join in the picnic lunch.

Our Dad is a great fan of picnics. He always wants to boil up water and make tea. The trouble is, that you have to do it on a little primus stove – that is a small portable stove that burns paraffin, once you can get it to light; you have to keep pumping it till it sprays up into a nice blue flame. And as you may have noticed, a beach can be a pretty windy place. So the primus stove keeps blowing out. Boiling a kettle of water can take ages.

So Dad comes up with an ingenious solution. He gets an old biscuit tin. One of the really old fashioned square shaped ones made of tin, that are about the size of a small stool. The primus stove fits neatly inside it, so it protects the flame from the wind. Dad even cut out a flap in one side, so he can reach in and operate the pump when it is needed.

So we get our tea a bit sooner!

Which helps if you're shivering with the cold!

Dad carving the Christmas turkey, with Sheila, Mum and Trevor. Paul must have taken the photo.

Christmas holidays are great as well, of course, especially when it's time for Christmas dinner. Like most other people, we always have a turkey for Christmas, and Dad likes to do the carving and serving at the table – like he does at picnics. I suppose it's a Dad thing.

And of course Christmas is for presents. I'm 10 years old now and Lego hasn't been invented yet. So for Christmas I get a set of Minibrix – which are very similar to Lego but made of hard red and white rubber, not plastic.

I spend a lot of time building things with Minibrix. It makes a change from my stamp-collecting.

And of course, little boys like me wear ties, even on Christmas Day and playing with Minibrix.

While little girls look on admiringly.

Well, in the adverts at least.

I don't think Grace Brown was very interested…

Getting Minibrix for Christmas

Chapter 7

Into my heart

'IS YOUR NAME IN THE LAMB'S BOOK OF LIFE?' my brother Paul asked me.

It was a Sunday and we had come home from church and Sunday School. That must have been what the minister had been talking about. But to be honest, I don't think I really knew what Paul meant. I think I was about six years old at the time. I remember the moment well, but I don't remember exactly when it was, except that I was still a wee boy in primary school.

'I'm not sure,' I probably replied.

'Well, you need to be,' says Paul. 'It means that Jesus knows your name and you belong to him and can go to be with him in heaven. In the Bible, 'The Lamb of God' is another name for Jesus.'

'So how can I be sure that my name is in his book?'

'All you have to do is pray to him,' says Paul. 'Just ask Jesus to come into your heart and forgive your sins and make you his child. And he promised that he will do that. And then you can be sure.'

So I did.

We were all taught to say our prayers before getting into bed each night, but I'd never prayed for that before. So I remember doing what Paul said one night at my bedside. I can't remember the exact words, but it was something like this,

> *'Dear Lord Jesus, please come into my heart. I know you died on the cross for me, so please forgive my sins. Please make me your child and put my name in your book. I want to belong to you now and be with you forever. Amen.'*

Well, nothing very exciting happened, but I knew from then on, and I still do, that Jesus did what I asked him. In fact, Jesus promises to do that for anybody who asks – however young or old. You can ask Jesus to come into your heart at any time of life, whatever age you are.

So now I know that I belong to Jesus. I know that he is in my life. Or rather, that my life is really being lived for him, and has been ever since that day. That's when I became not just the son of my Mum and Dad, but a child of God, a follower of Jesus, a Christian.

Now of course, I was still just a wee boy, but I'd grown up enough to know that asking Jesus to 'come into my heart' was not, like, him literally climbing inside my body! I knew that your '*heart*' is a way of talking about your own *life*, and about what is really important and special to you. I knew I was asking Jesus to just come in and be part of *me*.

When you really love somebody, you maybe write their name and draw a little heart beside it, with kisses and hugs! Or you send a text message with a red heart emoji. ♥

That's what you do when you send a birthday card to your Mum or Dad, or they give one to you. They're 'in your heart' and you are in their hearts.

They belong to you and you belong to them and that's a kind of love that is very, very special, right there 'in your heart'.

And when grown-ups 'fall in love' they send sloppy cards with love-hearts all over them – just to show how much they love each other. 'I love you with all my heart,' we whisper, with hugs and cuddles.

So having somebody 'in your heart' means they are right in the deepest and most important part of your life. Nobody matters more than a person who is 'in your heart.'

That's what I meant about Jesus, and I still do.

Well, we don't send cards with love-hearts on them to Jesus (though maybe that would be a good idea at Christmas!). But when I asked Jesus to come into my heart, I knew what it meant. It means that he loves me with all his heart, and I love him with all mine.

Asking Jesus to 'come and live in my heart' means that
- I want Jesus to be in my life,
- I want him to be at the centre of my life,
- I want him to guide and bless and control my life,
- I want to follow him, and do what he said, and live for him,
- for the whole of my life,
- and forever.

Well, it was a very simple prayer when I was just a child. But I know that I meant it. And God knew I meant it. And it has been the most important thing about my life ever since. And as I grew up into a bigger boy, and then a teenager, and then a student, and then a grown-up, and then a husband, and then a father, and finally Papa – that has always been what is right at the centre of my life.

It's actually what it means to be a Christian. A Christian is somebody who wants to belong to Jesus Christ and to follow him and learn from him. Of course, as I've grown older I understand a whole lot more about what being a Christian means. I've read a lot more books. I've gone to worship and thank God in many different churches. And I've learned a lot more about God and Jesus and the Bible. But it was that prayer I prayed as a little boy that started it all off, and I'm very glad about that.

Please forgive my sins, I prayed to Jesus. Well, I think maybe Jesus smiled at that!

I mean, I was only a wee lad, and anybody would say that my sins were not very many or terribly big! I wasn't old enough to do really big bad things. I was just a happy, sometimes cheeky, wee boy like all my friends.

But I was not stupid. I knew there were plenty of times when I did things, or said things, that were not good or even nice. Things that are not pleasing to God. Bad choices. Things I felt ashamed of. Things that hurt other people and made them sad – even people I loved. Things I wished I'd never done or said. There were plenty of those kind of bad things even in the middle of most of the time when I was just 'being good' at school, or playing with my friends, or laughing and fighting with my brother Trevor.

All of us do those kinds of things, don't we? Even grown-ups (especially grown-ups)! And it starts from when we're very young. It's so easy to get angry, or jealous, or selfish, or disobedient, or cross, or rude, isn't it? Sometimes it seems so much easier to tell a lie than tell the truth. Sometimes we just don't like other boys and girls and we say nasty things, or we hit out and hurt somebody else. Sometimes we even do that to our own family!

And sometimes we feel so ashamed, and we say 'Sorry,' and we really mean it. And other times we just put on a sorry face, or we say sorry just because we're told to, but we don't really feel very sorry inside.

Well, I was no different from all that some of the time. As I said, I wasn't stupid enough to think I was perfect!

And it all sort of comes out from inside us, doesn't it? Actually, that's what Jesus said one time. He said that it's from out of our hearts that all kinds of bad things come. It feels like sometimes you just can't stop what's inside you coming out (and I don't just mean when you're sick)! That bad thought becomes a bad word. That sudden feeling angry makes you hit out and yell at somebody else. It all starts inside, in your heart.

So I do remember thinking that, if Jesus was going to come and live in my heart, he would need to clean it up first. I remember that I had a picture in my mind that my life was a bit like a house, and my heart was at the centre of the house, like our kitchen or dining room where everything happened most of the time. So if Jesus was going to come in and live inside the house of my life, then he would have to clean away the dirty and bad things inside there. In fact, he would need to keep on doing that all the time, just like my Mum was always cleaning our house and making us kids do our chores.

So that's what I meant by asking Jesus to forgive my sins.

Come in and clean up my life-house! Then you can live there and keep it clean.

I also remember that when I prayed to Jesus by my bedside I thanked Jesus for dying on the cross for my sins. That's how I knew my sins, big or small or whatever they were, could be forgiven. I'd known that from as long as I could remember. I'm sure you do too. We know the Bible stories, at home and in church. So again and again (not just at Easter) we learn about the cross and we are told:

'Jesus died for our sins.'

What does that mean?

It means that, even though Jesus himself had done nothing wrong, he took all *our* wrong things on his own shoulders. Jesus had done no sin himself, but he suffered and died on the cross for *our* sins.

Well, that made sense to me. If Jesus had carried my sins on the cross, then my sins could be taken away and be forgiven. All the bad things could be dealt with and washed away. In fact, that's exactly what it felt like (and it still feels like this) – having them all 'washed away'. Like clearing out all the rubbish and dirt from the house and making it all nice and clean and fresh again. That's what it's like when your sins are forgiven by God.

And that was a great feeling! And it still is! When Jesus comes to live in your heart, he gives you a good wash – and he goes on doing that all through your life, because we go on needing it. I never ever stop being thankful to God that he forgives my sin and washes me clean again. It's for the whole of life!

Some years after I said that prayer, my Mum and Dad gave me a Bible of my own. It had very thin crinkly paper and a beautiful soft black leather cover and smelt lovely!

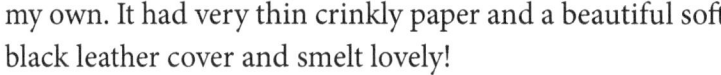

Of course, in those days it was the old King James Version, full of 'thee' and 'thou' and 'dost' and 'saith', and all that kind of old fashioned language. But people spoke like that in church when they prayed to God, so I mostly understood it (though I don't know why they thought they had to talk to God like that).

I have to say, though, that there are plenty of bits in the Bible that are pretty complicated and hard to understand – and that's true for me even now, not just when I was a little boy. But I loved my Bible and I still do. It 'speaks' words from God into my heart.

My Mum used to make me learn whole chapters of the Bible by heart. And when I could stand in front of her and recite a chapter word-perfect from memory, she would reward me by letting me choose any other book I liked and she would buy it for me. I learned Isaiah 53, John 14, Romans 12, and some of the Psalms by heart. Maybe that's why in later life I have studied the Bible a lot, and spend a lot of my life teaching and preaching from it in many different places round the world, and writing books to help people understand it better.

Jesus is in my heart, and the Bible is in my head!

The Bible is full of lots of stories, as I'm sure you know. But the Bible *as a whole* is like one great big single story. It tells God's big story, from the beginning of creation, to the future new creation when Jesus returns. It tells us that, even though we chose to disobey God, God still made a promise to Abraham that God would bless all nations on earth through his people. Then it tells the long story of that people, Israel in the Old Testament part of the Bible, preparing the way for Jesus and the stories of the Gospels. And then comes the story of how the first disciples (followers of Jesus) spread the good news far and wide, about the true God and his Son Jesus Christ. They told how Jesus died on the cross and rose again from the dead, how he is now reigning in heaven and will return to put all things right in the new creation, and how we need to believe and trust in him.

This whole big Bible story makes sense to me. It explains why so much bad stuff happens in the world. It tells us what God has done to save the world, through Jesus. It gives me hope for the future, in God's new creation. And it puts my own little life, as a wee Belfast boy now grown a lot older, safe into God's hands. I can play a tiny part in God's big story!

I'm sure that there was something else that helped me really understand the prayer I said that night. Something that helped me know what I meant when I asked Jesus to come into my heart. It was the picture that used to hang on my bedroom wall. Here it is. I still have it.

It's a picture of the seaside with boats and fishermen. Maybe that's why I love the sea so much, and especially rowing boats! On the back there is

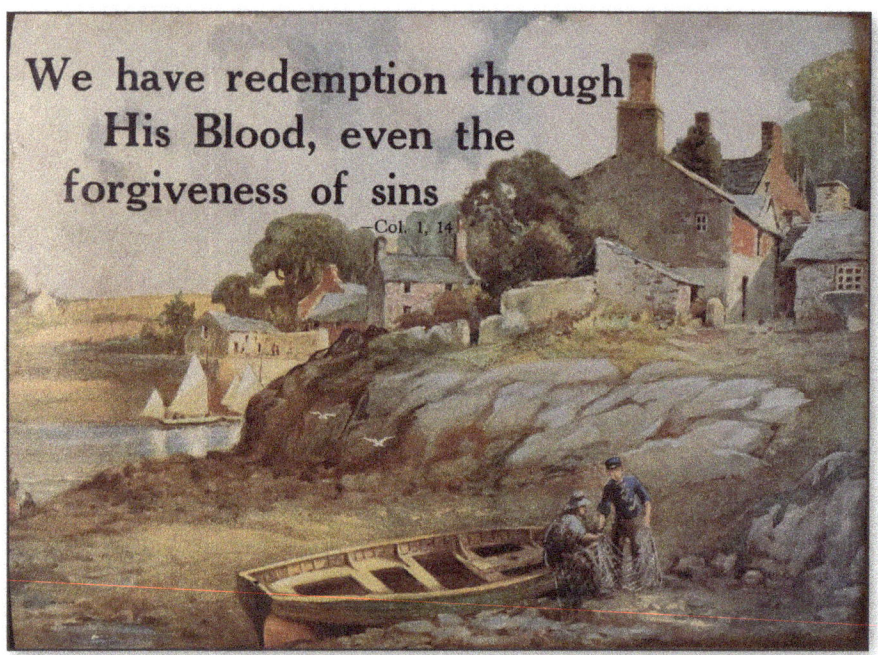

The picture that hung in my bedroom since I was 3 years old.

some faded writing. It says, 'To CHRISTOPHER, with much love for your 3rd birthday. From SHEILA and PAUL.' That means this picture was hanging on my bedroom wall from before I could even read!

But when I could read it, there was a verse from the Bible written on the picture. It was a verse about Jesus. It says,

> *'We have redemption through His Blood, even the forgiveness of sins'*
>
> Colossians 1:14

Now I knew that *'through his blood'* meant 'because Jesus died on the cross.' And somebody probably explained to me that *'redemption'* is just a big word that means being rescued or saved from danger or death. So that picture was silently telling me three very important things every day in my own little bedroom.

Three very wonderful things, actually.

Three things that I thank God for almost every day of my life:

1. That Jesus died on the cross and rose again.
2. That Jesus died so that my sins could be forgiven.
3. That because Jesus died for me, I am 'redeemed.' And that is like a kind of rescue. It is like I have been saved from danger, the danger of being separated from God. So I'm safe in God's hands and will live with Jesus forever.

Those are three very happy and beautiful things that I wish every child could know. For they can be true for anybody at any age, as Jesus promised. And all it takes is what my brother Paul told me to do when he explained to me about the Lamb's book of life. Pray to Jesus, ask him for forgiveness, and invite him into your life. And then go on following Jesus and living for him for the rest of your life.

Now then, if that bedroom picture was given to me on my 3rd birthday, on 9th October 1950, then it must have been only a few months after that in the summer of the following year, while I was still three, that that I had that other big rescue, where my story began.

It is the earliest thing in my life that I remember. That day on the farm when my Dad came rushing out and saved me from sinking into that pile of pig manure!

- Dad rescued me,
- then he washed me clean, and
- then he forgave me (I'm sure he did!).

And just a few years later, Jesus answered my prayer and did those same three things for me. He rescued me, washed me and forgave me – only much deeper than from a pile of pig manure!

Then he came into my heart and into my life to stay.

And that wee Belfast boy has belonged to Jesus ever since.

www.ingramcontent.com/pod-product-compliance
Lightning Source LLC
Chambersburg PA
CBHW060934170426
43194CB00024B/2958